Be Alone With Me

POETRY MOVES US

Be Alone With Me

POETRY MOVES US

LARRY GOLICZ

ARPress
ILLUMINATING IDEAS,
EMPOWERING VOICES

ARPress
45 Dan Road Suite 5
Canton, MA 02021
Hotline: 1(888) 821-0229
Fax: 1(508) 545-7580

Ordering Information:

Quantity sales. Special discounts are available on quantity purchases by corporations, associations, and others. For details, contact the publisher at the address above.

Printed in the United States of America.

ISBN-13:   Softcover   979-8-89330-903-4
               eBook   979-8-89330-904-1

Library of Congress Control Number: 2024902481

TABLE OF CONTENTS

CHAPTER IV

CHAPTER V

CHAPTER VI

CHAPTER VII

INTRODUCTION

*A*s with prayer, poetry moves us. A gift, it represents our innermost feelings, a sensitivity about life, nature, and emotions that reach down into our soul. It then brings us back to ourselves better than we started. You feel, hear, and see the many wonders of being, captured in time, distilled into its purest, reflective, crystalline form. At one moment it rescues you, the next it will deliver you with inspiration, and elevates you from where you started.

DEDICATION

All of my poems, written over the last thirty years, and collected and edited for this book, are dedicated to my family, and my friends, especially my brother Kenny, my wife Peggy, my sons and their wives and our grand children.

CHAPTER I

INCURABLE ROMANTIC

*O*ne of the most rewarding emotions in life is love. It can be expressed in many warm and delicate ways to anchor our hearts with meanings that keep us going for life. My poems express love in all of its greatness while engendering the joys, sadness, as well as the easy and hard parts of living for and with those we love.

A GENTLE BREEZE WALKING ALONE

It feels good caressing my face,
Teasing my soul with a gentle lace.
Lightly swaying, a graceful walk,
I attend the wind as if we talk.

My soul distills love's senses,
Smiles hidden by formal fences.
Its laugh now echoes in my heart.
It calls me back when we're apart.

THE DISCOVERY OF LOVE

By Chance, You Know, A Friend Fixed Date,
We All Seem Seeking Love Bug's Bate.
Eyes Wide Open, We Speak To Meet.
Then In Haste, We Smile 'n Take a Seat.

From Moments Then, We Yearn to Say,
"How Are You?" (I'm Lonely Today.)
And Then That Way We Seek Our Fate.
And Hope Our Move Is Not Too Late.

Slowly, Frightfully So, You Know,
Our Love Comes Out, That Way Aglow,
Trembling, And With God's Grace We Pray,
Our Meeting Hearts, Will Feel That Way.

And When It's Two, Who Play This Fool,
True Love Is Bound, To Be Less Cruel.
In Fact This Love, Is Greater Than,
The Greatest Of The Greatest Then.

It's Lasting Sense, Forever Mine?
It Ends Up One, In Life Sublime.

On A Bench, With Evening's Dew,
A Lighthouse Beam, Shines Clear For You.

*"Could We Be, Our Love Strong and True, Our
Lifetime Offered Through and Through?
Like Doves, We'll Nest, And Sing Our Coo.
My Wife, My Husband, We Say I Do"*

HANDS THAT SPEAK

Tendered caress in light, apart,
Touching softly for life to start.
Our sense of time will lose its bounds,
With knowing eyes and whispered sounds.
With trust in love, our hands hold fine,
It's knowing then our hearts combine,
To share our lives in fear or joy,
Hands forever last, firm not coy.
Till the light that comes to greet us,
In the arms of the Lord who meets us.

BE MY VALENTINE

I dreamed moonlight bathing your face,
Of your eyes, shining, I am fond.
I dreamed your soul, a song, a place,
A timeless secret and our bond.

I dreamed my soul's endless pleasure,
Harbored safely in your arms,
Gently touched without measure,
Pressed so softly with your charms.

Awakened now, my dream is true.
I know my love, I know it's you.

THE WHITE ROSE

Purity is our love in hand.
Secret and innocent we stand.
Side by side we honor anew,
Our life for two each year, ...I do.

MY MOTORCYCLE LADY

There is no rider so tender,
Her warming hugs from the fender,
A closeness she does not conceal,
It's a oneness no one can steal.

Open air surrounds our seeing,
Making us one within our being.
The rumbling pipes confirm our thought.
We smile with glee the time we caught.

From time to time, each place we've been,
We relish all the places seen.
As we take curves and laugh on side,
In sun or cold the trails we tried.

In a few moments, shocked with fear,
Bound us close so closely dear.
But turn the key and you will see,
My biker babe is there with me.

HANDS HOLDING FAST, LAST FOREVER

Hands held tender, in light and dark,
Span the deep time our lives will mark.
With knowing eyes and whispered sounds

Hands holding fast with joy abounds.
Hands held firm, join the soul to know
the world, wherever you may go.

No greater gift, held on this way,
To give and take the same each day.
God Bless and Keep These Hands, To Stay.

LOVE'S LEAD

My path seemed clear to me.
Your smile was there to see.

Love's leading where it goes,
Somewhere to stay, it knows.

It is the place so true.
It's all I want, it's you.

Now you're gone, I'm so blue,
Alone, my love is still for you.

I long for your tenderness,
Your smile, and a caress.

Here is my place with you.
It's all I want, it's true.

WATCHING A CAMP FIRE

Dancing Flames Prompt Silly Mind Games,
Whispers of Love with Foreign Names,
A Fantasy with all its Joy,
Jokes and Laughs like a glowing toy.

Wales Come Forth from Burning Embers.
Sighs So Long with Stringy Members.
Escaping Minds It Really Saves.
Now Camp Fires Light Our Hearts with Plays.

Warmth in Embers and Flames with Fame,
All Dreams of Life For Us to Claim,
Camp Fires Breed Best While Aging On.
Still Burning on From Dawn to Dawn.

THE GIRL IN THE REAR VIEW MIRROR

Turning the key, new life this way,
Hard at my car's wheel for the day
Then cars stopped, she saw me at bay.

Rear mirror, facing with her smile,
Some traffic lurching, moves awhile,
Hope pushing me back to her file.

Rear smile, her smile, haunting my way,
But traffic on and traffic sway,
Timid, this boy, lost her that day.

I looked once more. Saw her retreat.
Moved on again. Looked to the street.
The mirrored girl, I dared to meet.

FOREVER WITH YOU

In a dream as it seems,
Alone as if unseen,
Lost in fear, hands held out,
See my hand, turn about.

Find your way, for another day.
I'm here with you, to stay,
Our love combined for sure,
Shall with God, always endure.

CHAPTER II

KEEP ON TRUCKING

*B*eing a boater and a biker, taking risks of life and limb goes with the effort. We lead with our chins at times because we want the excitement and the awakening of our skills to perform in a world filled with challenges and danger.

A BIKERS POEM

Brake lights finding near darkness still,
A biker roams beyond the hill.
Etched against a late setting sun,
He finds the turn and leans for fun.

A windward rush, a hardened heal,
Legs wrapped around a frame of steel,

Guiding light, with a gleam of chrome
He presses on with daring shown.

The pavement rises, rolls, and lists,
Charging strong with dangerous twists.
It whips the wheels from side to side,
And tempts the biker with his pride.

Faster still, till the engine roars,
Humbling thrill, no simple, passing chores,
Testing fate, the Matador turns,
Touching pavement, his kneecap burns.

Caressing still each curve with lust,
He presses on with blinded trust.
With metal arms that cradle his soul,
The biker moves with bike as whole.

A BOATERS PRAYER IN A STORM

Black water boiling, foiling might,
Churning, lapping, capping at night,
My boat plunges from wave to wave,
The motor's surge looks to behave.

This wave, next wave, all command fear,
Turning my bow from front to rear.
Up goes my stern, exposing rudder,
Engines roaring, with a shudder.

Then there's one wave for sure the best,
From deepest trough to highest crest.
Its sure to shake a pilot's knees,
For all I asks is dear God, please.

With fear I pray my courage holds,
To steer my boat and make me bold.
To get me home safe and sound,
The waves already gained my pound

THE SURFER

Float gently, the warm winds, ever washing
With pearly waves,
Smoothed With light from the moon,
Applauding my soul.

Then lift me, dash me down, mountains
Capped in white,
With blinding light from the sun,
With no horizon.

Closer and closer to my face they come.
Greeting me to fly into their
cradled lap, as I tunnel into eternity
and hold my breath.

I rise high beyond my mere existence,
As if I never existed before,
Without fear of end.

I climbed upon the largest wave trembling,
Riding me above the world to the sky,
I proclaimed my arrival with a smile.

MY PHYSICAL STRESS TEST

Getting ready, held in a room,
Waiting steadily full of doom,
Will I pass the treadmill, or last,
Or glow all wrong on X-rays cast?

I pray the stress does not me best,
Running the gauntlet is the test.
Starting slow is the way we go.
Getting fast, I hope I can show.

Taking blood and what's my pressure,
Keep on running, not for leisure.
One more time, on the highest climb,
I keep on running, just in time.

Oh finally, the mill is off.
Now I stop to wheeze, hack, and cough.
Then to wait for just one more turn,
To scan my heart, can't move, so stern.

When all is done I've had no fun.
It's not a game that starts a gun.
But well I know it's meaning to me,
To hear the doctor, it's wait- and- see.

LIVING ON

With time and place and all in space,
Then here we are with life to face.
Then thinking, what to do?
We simply say we live as you.

As time goes on. we ask again.
With more or little less as then.
We thread our way to make a weave.
We go on living. Some believe.

Wherever oceans create a wave,
They go on rolling strong and brave.
by living now, I'll reach somehow.
For great or small, we all shall fall.

Heard everywhere all the time,
I hold my hands and stand in line.
There is no failure, nor success.
With living life I do my best.

FREE LANCING

Piercing the veil, I'm on my way,
Up there always, wanting to stay,
Peeking, seeking a brighter day,
Ever pushing the end of play.

Searching, I know, for times aglow,
With endless chanting, on-the-go.
Double time and sweating for the gold,
Running, waiting, then tired and cold?

Fearless to reach success is bold,
Always dreaming of new tales told,
Failing flows quickly down the sink,
Just a stop for another think.

Coming and going, best to tell,
The journey's worth ringing the bell.
If no bid is made for a win,
There is no past to where I've been.

WE MUST HAVE WORDS

Over the long day of telling,
We often use words of selling.
It's not that life is ours to blame.
We will sow our words without shame.

Alone today, we may shout our way,
With words alive we need to say,
Our thoughts dissolve from grim to grey,
then pure and slick, they save each day.

We must have words to warm our hearts.
We must have words to shoot like darts.
We must have words to clear our minds.
We must have words to know all kinds.

So words it is, shallow or deep?
Our souls shall sieve the words to keep.
With no empty bleating to share,
We leap beyond for those we dare.

Life in the Fast Lane

Life in the fast lane goes to fame.
Its Leader Board has name on name,
All for fun or a solemn game?
Dare we must, or be proven lame!

So if we trip, or stop to wait,
Will life then baulk and close the gate?
It's sure to prove we can't be late,
Or choose now to accept our fate.

Move on then, with no distractions.
Remove life from like's contraptions.
When seeing something on the side,
Keep on going, as if it died.

So travel on and pass it by.
The meaning of life is much to try.
And cherish it now, hold it dear.
For the meaning of life is always near.

WORKING THE FENDER LINE

Endless fenders march to address,
Lift, and place with no mental stress.
Each day is the same as before,
Hope I make it, or take the door.

In numbness, complying is hard,
When trapped to play, just one card.
Yet pay's good, as I know it should,
But life is dull and feels like wood.

Overtime makes me better than most.
But my feelings grow hard as toast.
My family smiles, life seems good.
While working the line, as I should,

The trade is made, and I give it my all.
Man on the line, I never stall.
My mind holds on, for dreams to keep
While all my drinking helps me sleep.

THE TREE

See that tree rooted in the sky,
Keeping the earth from falling by.
Its strong branches of silver gray,
Make me calm on a stormy day.

I hope that tree will never die.
If it's life's anchor, I will try.
I'll make myself no walk away,
When heaven falls that tree will stay.

Yes, unseen strength in roots below,
Do wed the earth to sky to show
A secret in the welding ground
By holding long for us around.

Yes, with this tree I lead my life,
To make it through marching with fife,
It gives me strength, a path to see,
Then, all secured as one for me.

CHAPTER III

EASY ON ME

*F*rom day to day, our memories curiously entertain us with how things happened giving us time to reminisce. Sometimes a happening creates new paths of appreciation about life. Indeed, our world is the stuff of memories and with them we survive to begin each day. Stop and take some time to marvel about it. In doing it you will care to think about it in a meaningful and happy if not marveled way.

THE LARK

Past twelve it is, noting a scowl,
A cat on prowl in search of fowl?
My ears now keen to hear the scene,
My window where the sound had been.

A lark is stirring, a simple bird,
makes a sound, a scornful word.
What made this bird sing out, I fear,
A note at night so close to hear?

A tree branch shakes and goes around.
A cat I think falls to ground.
No trumpet shrill or bird is tossed.
Sweet sound of night, no lark is lost.

CALM WAVES

Evening shines like day that way,
Peaceful and free from fuss and fray.
Glassy waves, just lapping to time,
Layered with curves, line upon line.

Greeting the sand gently with tunes,
Glistening still, these dancing dunes.
Waves come to shore and back away,
To tease the sand to come or stay.

Waves watch the man who wanders near,
To coax him close to be sincere.
They bathe his feet in cooling night.
And wish him well, his dream's delight.

LJG September 20, 2008

SAND CASTLES ON THE BEACH

Wave upon Wave can Build the Sand,
Rippled and Hard before my Hand.
To Scoop it Firm to Stack a Pile,
I Build my Castle with an Ample Style.

Turrets and Walls with Towered Keep,
Motes fill with Water not so Deep,
And I Marvel the Bridge Across,
My Mote without Water Loss.

But then the Waves come Creeping in,
To Wash away my Castle's Yin.
Creating so much Endless Play,
I Sigh, Dear Castle, Melting Away.

And then, I Watch my Son with Fun.
Building His Castle in the Sun,
Smiling over a Clever Wall,
Then Seeing Waves Washing it All.

For him the Joy is still to Care,
For Making Castles with so much Flare.
Even though he knows it is Lost,
He keeps building despite the Cost.

And Joy again does come to Bare.
My Grandson now is Building There.
He Struggles hard to make his Mark.
Castles cast light to end his Dark.

With shining eyes, his future's Cast.
Castles place him before the Mast,
To See the World with Dreamy Eyes,
and build more Castles in the Skies

I FEEL LIKE A PUDDLE

Today I fell like a flat puddle,
Sliding slowly through a day's muddle,
Always clear, laid out and fluid,
I ease my way like a druid.

Lacking in form, there is no fear,
Taking on things so tall, so near.
Overhead storms wash them all out,
Still my puddle remains strong and stout.

Do step in my puddle, you will see,
All in the world that all can be.
There is a place in my puddle face.
Reflecting life, with all its space.

DREAMER

The song of life begins, it seems,
With wishes made to lasting dreams,
A dream of life, lived far away,
dancing, smiling, singing all day.

So, lift me up, go dream of mine.
Carry me high, beyond this time.
Leaping quick, with spiraling light,
Pausing, darting, beyond the night.

Startling brightness, shimmering gold,
No shadows darken stairways bold,
Touching the glamour, feeling its power,
Deafened by chanting, hour to hour,

As time goes on, dreams may wear out.
Torn and tattered, yet always stout.
Changing faces, somewhere daily,
Go where laughing, all so gaily.

MUSIC TO MY EARS

The flute that whispers sound so near,
And stirs the mind to hear so clear,
The violin that sings with wings,
With angel's notes, it does those things.

Piano keys may softly stroke,
Or pound like thunder as if broke,
Then turns the sound to smiles so wide,
Its joy revealed for us inside.

Longing still to glide on through space,
The music carries place to place,
Then gently settles to itself down,
Lightly breezed with a golden crown.

DOVES MAKING A HOME

Sipping wine, I stared at the sky.
As drifting dreams dulled my mind's eye,
A dove flew to a tree branch tie.
A second came and cooed a sigh.

They cooed approval, this site best
For the home of their children's nest.
First one twig then two, after each coo,
The two worked till the forming dew.

Each morning I waited their coo.
And my ears affirmed feelings true.
Then one day no sound or dove there.
And as I looked the nest was bare.

Day to day searching sky and grounds,
Not embarrassed, I yearned for sounds,
To find the doves, for whom I care.
Hoping, no cat had scared them there.

Did the babies fly out of sight?
Did they migrate on a long flight?
I know that I miss them true.
Their mated love and soothing coo.

A HORNET ON AN AIRPORT WAITING ROOM GLASS WINDOW

Sturdy limbed very smart and fast,
A hornet landed on my glass.
Close to my eyes on the other side
It stared at me, as if it cried.

Was it praying for its lost soul?
Or resting its way, on the go?
Antennae down ready to sprint,
Its steady stare gave me no hint.

It moved a bit to stretch its wings
Then it danced around weaving rings,
It cleared its heart, of lonely things?
And saved its soul from lasting stings?

Still staring, I think it is kind,
Musing over my face to find,
Meaning or wonder from inside.
Turning its head, it looked aside?

In turn my head tilted to pose.
It tilted back as if it knows,
To show me why so small it is,
Can teach a life, so well it lives.

I wonder why its staring still?
Its telling me my heart to fill,
born new by its quiet purview,
sharing its soul through and through?

There is my plane and I must leave,
My friend, I wish, was on my sleeve.
I wish it the best through the glass,
glad at a sight I did not pass.

FRESH FLOWERS ALONG A ROAD

An Asphalt Track Goes Front to Back
With White Specs Now Zipping Through Black.
This Numbing Speed Makes my Mind Bleed,
But Going on is What I Need.

Then Comes a Split I Dare Not Miss.
A Change of Pace Much Like a Kiss.
From Crippled Pavement to Smooth Curbs,
My Eyes now Wonder in the Burbs.

Then Stop and Go is Oh so Slow.
I Start to Looking, Just to Know.
A White Cross I Saw Kept with Care.
And I Cried a Tear as I Stare.

For Love Blossoms Fully in May
Fresh Flowers Made it so That Day.

A SHORT WINTER BLIZZARD IN THE CITY

A cold day begins that way, a chilling
damp wind on
A grey formless sky joined seamless with
the horizon.
The city awakens muscles, and stiffens its resolve,
Pumping up its captured corpuscles to firmly
devolve.

It beats a sullen drum, fast, relentless,
stern that way.
Under its yoke we make our way most
every day.
We feed with frenzy and fire our souls
with drunken goals.
Despite the cold, wind and even snow, the city goes.

Nature, not brutal, cruel, or bizarre offers breezes.
Comes a blizzard, the city wheezes, sometimes
sneezes.
Brash, bold, it still pushes on until the end
is told.
"Workers go home now before you can't."
My streets do fold.

So home we go in the snow, and labor
twice that day.
But joy, not pain treats smiles and cold teeth, as
children play.
For dad and mom are home today, a snowman is
built.
There is no schedule to keep, no shopping trip or
guilt.

Smell the freshened air and pace the white crystals
you know.
See the forms on the trees just like made angels of
snow.
Then soft howls of snowflakes brush across the field
so clear.
Thank nature for this respite, a peace we seldom
hear.

Our work waits, while snow ploughs stack the snow
to clean the streets.
There's our play in a dirty heap, meant to quell our
treats.
Bored with stillness, the city yawns still wanting us
late.
Then the City calls all back, and the next snow we
wait.

JUNK YARD JUNGLE
(Warning: Dogs Released at Closing)

Treasure Hunting is for the Fame.
Just finding Parts is in the Game.
A Glint of Chrome, You Know the Name,
Fifty-Nine Chrysler, Tortured Lame.

Getting Part's another Story,
Fighting Wasps, just for the Glory?
Taking your Hammer and Lever,
Prying Doors rusted forever.

Grasping a Power Window Part,
You Toss the Motor in the Cart.
Knowing Its Fifty-Five Years Old,
You've found a Treasure, Good as Gold.

Getting back before they Close Gates,
You see Piled Cars, await their Fates.
One part from them, Preserves their Day,
Junkyard Junkers, save them that Way.

THE HUB CAP MAN

On Old Highways, There's Always Still
A Hub Cap Man, with Age and Will.
He Carries on to Claim His Fame,
Caps from Wheels of Every Name.

A Wanderer by Breed and Voice,
The Hub Cap Man Still Hunts His Choice.
And Mounts His Chrome, A Choir of Light,
Thousands Shown on Fences in Flight.

Though Age and Time Have Made Him Slow,
There is No Place He will not Go.
For Hub Caps are His Treasure True.
And Living Life is All to Do.

The Hub Cap Man Will Always Be,
The Man Who Finds the Truth to See.
Hub Caps Reflect Our Chrome and Glee
God Bless the Hub Cap Man for Me.

TIME WAS TIME WHEN

So clear to be, it was to me.
The time that was like now you see.
When I was young and so sincere,
It is like now, just then and here.

My eyes are closed, as was that day.
I best recalled, a wish that way.
When I am with her then to say,
We live again as best we may.

Going now with no sense of past,
For what was then, we still will last.
The joys we knew were many too,
And living on we want to do.

MISSED FRIENDS

Landscapes of life uninvited,
Somehow making me delighted.
And for this, reason has no say,
All pictures appear as they may.

Is time so willful, just a fling?
It comes then goes on flapping wing.
I think though, these frames of my mind,
Offered lame, a regretful kind.

I miss my friends of long ago.
I didn't know then, how well I know.
They were my friends for me so well,
Gone friends today can ring that bell.

I missed the past till time did tell.
It's now the way to see it well.

CHAPTER IV

RELFECTIONS AND DREAMS

Some times we find ourselves just floating aimlessly
like jetsam and flotsam in a sea of humanity.
Sometimes we dream of new paths and with them we
survive to begin each day.

MY TIME MACHINE

Time now and then comes back to mend,
A broken mirror without end,
The terms of love, and push and shove,
Yesterday's upside down, above.

All for real then, when I was five,
And smelling weeds and woods alive,
Even when twelve, I played so well,
With sticks, stones, and stories to tell.

Today, again my mind so clear,
When old is cold, and waiting dear,

When still I play, but less that way,
The time is then, and now today.

Often recalled a picture still,
Colors and smells a mind to fill,
I wonder how I lost them then,
But now receive and hold again.

Time has no past, with future last.
It takes the past to make a cast,
Then to sway in a lazy breeze,
And still again with frightful ease.

Yes, time is moving front to back,
And back again in a single track.
With frames of motion frozen still,
In striking portraits meant to fill.

Landscapes of my life invited,
Somehow make me so delighted.

And for this, reason offers play,
And pictures appear as they may.

So time is willful, just a fling?
It comes and goes, a flapping wing.
I think though, these frames of my mind,
Offer pain, a regretful kind.

I miss my friends of long ago.
We did so well without a show.
I missed their past, so time did tell.
It's now the way, to see it well.

SECRETS OF LIFE

A weighted mind, rushing with thought,
Shifts, blames, as it's endlessly caught,
Like howling, hot, sandpaper wind,
Chained to itself, how has it sinned?

Forming self in mindless chatters,
Cry saintly, then a stroke scatters
Preening as much, with holy rites,
An image of wandering knights.

Clutching at jokes, mocking the blind,
I long for signs, evil or kind,
Claiming to see, the why of me,
Seeking a clue, groping to be.

Secrets of life seek no reward,
Secrets revealed dampen the sword,
No treasures gained, no others claimed.
Meaning to me, not to be feigned.

THE ART OF APPRAISING LIFE

Appraising life can be hazy.
Some say it's crystal ball crazy.
No matter how a life lumbers,
Certainly there will be blunders.

When upon some conclusions made,
The given stand gets held and weighed.
Indeed, the life's work must be paid,
Or just get tossed or gently laid.

Appraising life's surely like sailing,
With life's wind changes prevailing.
And justly knowing that one could,
As always, is the case, one should.

So cheered, life that starts with a smile,
Travels with lust, mile after mile.
For life is never couldn't say could.
For those who try, you know they would.

SLEEPLESS

Head on my pillow, rest for tonight,
Then closing my eyes, seeking some flight.

Touching to soothe a marsh mellow soft
on a pure white sleigh cruising aloft.

Loving those hours, in silence, with sleep,
Tired with nothing to feel in the deep.

Cold in my face, and dead in my limbs,
My mind awakens thinking of sins.

At once chasing, then falling down lost,
I fear this sleep without the fair wake.

With the fate of my dreams what's the cost.
Ending with that life, what have I lost?

CHAPTER V

DEALING WITH REALITY

*L*ife on the inside can be a lot different from life on the outside. In the world at large, from place to place, country to country, and culture to culture, we end up measuring the differences from our inside to the reality of the outside.

HOW THINGS CAN END

How to die the man did cry,
A willing way to make him sigh?
Burning, falling, bleeding out loud,
Or just jousting upon a cloud?

Turn his mind, this lofty prancer,
Not cancer, a bawdy answer,

Eaten to twigs and sulfur breath,
Leaving nothing but ignoble death.

Flying on high to falling low,
Surely that's a fun way to go,
Thinking stinking and mess to show.
Better to try and be a pro.

Speed is great and it just won't wait.
A cycle's roar is just plain great.
A skidding slide then jump of flight,
And flying again out of sight.

Or diving in water clear and blue,
Holding down, narcosis will do.
Or meet a shark happily eating,
Not nice nor easily beaten.

In war, for him there's no concern.
Death is likely easy to earn.
Just plain done remains for me.
Any death ends the fun you see.

THE BATTLE OF FREDERICKSBURG IN 1862

The river's other side, our goal,
A broken bridge, needs to be whole.
Foggy Morning, we need to cross.
With planks in hand, we fear no loss.

But shots rang out from Grays in town. The minis
zinged and whizzed around. We turned and ran to
save our lives.
But ordered back, we took the prize.

Face to face we took the town,
To find ourselves on lower ground.
Then across a swamp, Lee's men stood.
We charged them there and shot them good.

Then uphill to a field in Gray,
There a stone wall, where they would stay.
Their cannon rained its deadly shot,
Among our bodies soon to rot.

As muskets fired, we could not stop,
From rank to rank to reach the top.
Our bodies fell to form a shield
For men who tried and would not yield.

We charged till night, then laid to die.
Amid our groans, oh God, we cry.
Grays shot us down to bloody ground.
The charge had failed, no glory found.

Yes, well and good for those who stood.
To try again as best they could.
But, thousands fell, and then what then?
We crossed the river, back again.

Come hear us now our silent sound
Of men whose lives are in the ground.
It is our home for losses made.
This war is worth the price we paid.

THE TRUTH OF HONOR

At heights of glory, hear a horn.
A badge is worn, to show adorn.
A simple medal, made of tin.
To fight to win, it's not a sin.

Drums beat loudly to show the path.
Away with credence, hardened math.
Three lost but you stood tall and true,
To die that day, others do and do.

For honor's burden proudly worn,
With flags, guns and swords so borne.
No man talks honor without guilt,
Friends fought brave, for tombstones built.

They gave a life to carry on.
With its meaning, one goes beyond,
The daily bread, some wine and song,
To honor's trust and caring strong.

Honor's dreaming, moves along,
It carries the day, when all's gone.
Then nothing matters, but this song,
The hymn of battle for right, not wrong.

09 11 2014 18:46

A WALK ON TIANANMEN SQUARE

A mammoth square with gigantic faces
Carried by monks, parading in places,
Then standing front to back like numbered cows,
A wall of blank faces, praising Mao's.

Now empty, silent, somber, I strolled.
"A kite to fly for fun today? I'm told.
A crippled old man offered to sell it.
"Challenge yourself and fly freedom a bit!"

Why not buy the small kite, I dared.
My kite pressed the wind, I so cared.
Now zipping, halting, with a long tail laced,
Then screaming when Mao's statue dead faced.

Still searching, proud and free, it moved.
Too close to a giant red flag, people bowed.
Flapping heavy, the flag made a thunder.
The wind sighed, and the kite fell under.

It halted in contempt, and fell jerking.
As if fighting off some danger lurking,
It dropped, then weaved against a dimming sky,
It squirmed and twisted, fighting not to die.

Dropping to earth with shallow glooms,
Feared lost, I save my brave kite's runes.
Although my kite just fell from all its might
Held high, its spirit shines to make life right.

Suddenly, a boy runs and takes my string.
Smiling, he knows the kite for him would sing.
Lips stubbornly set, holding it he gleamed.
No monks on file could fight the kite he dreamed.

CHAPTER VI

SOUL SEARCHING

We make decisions about right and wrong, truth versus outright lies, sacrifices made for real or not, and cultural standards of correctness which may or may not be correct with internal standards and ethos. In the end it is a matter of religious beliefs and standards of behavior.

CALL IT CHRISTMAS FOR YOU AND ME

There is a star for you and me,
A star to show our way, you see.
At times of deceit and ill fame,
We seek to see a brighter name.

Those times are here, and full of fear,
Loud jeers and protests stealing cheer.
For Christmas is no longer said,
Nor may we see a baby's bed.

All at stake, our beliefs in us,
They conceal our hearts with such fuss.
Times in Bethlehem were the same,
When Romans came branding their name.

As now, they rule, without God's law,
Destroy morals, ethics, and awe.
Like Rome, they stand in their place,
As long as Rome carries the mace.

And Rome did fall in all its gall.
From deceit and lies and selfish law.
So where are we to go to be,
A Christian heart and Christmas free?

Go back to Congress, Courts, and He.
We need to show our vote to be.
Bring back Jesus for all to see.
And call it Christmas for you and me.

The Come Back Jesus

Where is God? Is Jesus now dead?
Born he died, for the world he bled.
Freed us from a secular head,
Where wisdom dies and faith turns lead.

Now we struggle to keep Him alive,
Their bullets aimed to make Him dive.
They know so little and claim so much,
and never felt his warming touch.

The fight goes on with right and wrong
Our Jesus lives, we sing his song.
Yes, falling now, we'll see them keep,
To caves of darkness, holes so deep.

Jesus knows them as his lost sheep,
Wandering packs that sleep and eat.
Bold with gun, but numb and dumb.
Bleating lies of how far they've come.

The climb to light can be a fright.
The face of God is worth the fight.
For hearts of most, I make this boast
You cannot live, beyond the host.

MY PRAYER

Lord my Lord of All,
Oh Lord my God Above,
Hear my Song in Stillness.
Hear by Me All my Love.

Lead Me from my Doubting,
The Darkness of my Soul.
Bring Me to your Gladness,
The Lord, My God, I know.

Lord My Lord of All,
Oh, Lord my God Above,
Take my Soul and Hold Me.
Lift my Heart with Your Love.

Lead Me from my Sadness,
The Starkness of my Soul.
Bring Me to your Gladness,
The Lord, My God, I know.

Lord my Lord of All,
Oh Lord, My God, Above,
Thank You for my Seeing,
All my Heart and Being

Your Will is Mine to Make

In Line with Christ, His Sake.
Give to All His Blessings
For All His Love to Take.

Lord my My Lord of All,
Oh, Lord my God Above.
Hear my Song in Stillness
Hear by Me All my Love.

CHAPTER VII

HAIKU POETRY

Japanese traditional Haiku has three lines in a poem in a 5/7/5 syllable count without rhymes and focusing on imagery from nature

Calm Sea Meets the Shore
Lapping Sounds on Sand Smoothed
Sings Peace for Ages.

The Doves Coo Morning
Breaks the Sun, Mountain High
Rays of Light Praying.

A Tree's Arm Reaching
The Green Leaves Wrapped Closely
Lures the Wind Gently.

The Misty Sky Blue
Soft to Touch No Sound or Fear
Embraces My Heart.

Rests My Eyes Silent
With a Smile Contented Be
Calming Waters Sea.
Sun Setting Fire Red

Round on a Glassy Plain Far
Mends the Day's Ending
LJG SEPTEMBER 29, 2008

DAYS OF FAWNS

Fawns silent, stretching
In rays of gold splashed green
Hasten steps, then look.

Eyes blinking, ears stiff
They swiftly turn to dancing
Circles of mirth and joy.

Prancing lightly clouds,
Antlers soon to crown repose,
Rising strong fawns go.

And furtive does skirt,
With pledges made for two,
Stand as fawns before.